AF589875

Table of Contents

method of preserving food from spoilage by storing it in containers that are hermetically sealed and then sterilized by heat. The process was invented after prolonged research by Nicolas Appert of France in 1809, in response to a call by his government for a means of preserving food for army and navy use. Appert's method consisted of tightly sealing food inside a bottle or jar, heating it to a certain temperature, and maintaining the heat for a certain period, after which the container was kept sealed until use. It was 50 years before Louis Pasteur was able to explain why the food so treated did not spoil: the heat killed the microorganisms in the food, and the sealing kept other microorganisms from entering the jar. In 1810 Peter Durand of England patented the use of tin-coated iron cans instead of bottles, and by 1820 he was supplying canned food to the Royal Navy in large quantities. European canning methods reached the United States soon thereafter, and that country eventually became the world leader in both automated canning processes and total can production. In the late 19th century, Samuel C. Prescott and William Underwood of the United States set canning on a scientific basis by describing specific time-temperature heating requirements for sterilizing canned foods. Originally, cans consisted of a sheet of tin-plated iron that was rolled into a cylinder (known as the body), onto which the top and bottom were manually soldered. This form was replaced in the early 20th century by the modern sanitary, or open-top, can, whose constituent parts are joined by interlocking folds that are crimped, or pressed together. Polymer sealing compounds are applied to the end, or lid, seams, and the body seams can be sealed on the outside by soldering. The modern tin can is made of 98.5 percent sheet steel with a thin coating of tin (i.e., tinplate). It is manufactured on wholly automatic lines of machinery at rates of hundreds of cans per minute. Most vegetables, fruits, meat and dairy products, and processed foods are stored in tin cans, but soft drinks and many other beverages are now commonly stored in aluminum cans, which are lighter and do not rust. Aluminum cans are made by impact extrusion; the body of the can is punched out in one piece from a single aluminum sheet by a stamping die. This seamless piece, which has a rounded bottom, is then capped with a second piece as its lid. Canneries are usually located close to the growing areas of the product to be packed, since it is desirable to can foods as quickly as possible after harvesting. The canning process itself consists of several stages: cleaning and further preparing the raw food material; blanching it; filling the containers, usually under a vacuum; closing and sealing the containers; sterilizing the canned products; and labeling and warehousing the finished goods. Cleaning usually involves passing the raw food through tanks of water or under high-pressure water sprays, after which vegetable or other products are cut, peeled, cored, sliced, graded, soaked, pureed, and so on. Almost all vegetables and some fruits require blanching by immersion in hot water or steam; this process softens the vegetable tissues and makes them pliable enough to be packed tightly, while also serving to inactivate enzymes that can cause undesirable changes in the food before canning. Blanching also serves as an additional or final cleansing operation.The filling of cans is done automatically by machines; cans are filled with solid contents and, in many cases, with an accompanying liquid (often brine or syrup) in order to replace as much of the air in the can as possible. The filled cans are then passed through a hot-water or steam bath in an exhaust box; this heating expands the food and drives out the remaining air; thus, after sealing, heat sterilizing, and cooling the can, the contraction of the contents produces a partial vacuum within the container. Certain products are vacuum-packed, whereby the cans are mechanically exhausted by specially designed vacuum-can sealing machines.Immediately after the cans are exhausted, they are closed and sealed; a machine places the cover on the can, and the curl on the can cover and the flange on the can body are rolled into position and then flattened together. The thin layer of sealing compound originally present in the rim of the cover is dispersed between the layers of metal to ensure a hermetic seal. The sealed cans are then sterilized; i.e., they are heated at temperatures high enough and for a long enough time to destroy all microorganisms (bacteria, molds, yeasts) that might still be present in the food contents. The heating is done in high-pressure steam kettles, or cookers, usually using temperatures around 240° F (116° C). The cans are then cooled in cold water or air, after which they are labeled. Canning preserves most of the nutrients in foods. Proteins, carbohydrates, and fats are unaffected, as are vitamins A, C, D, and B2. The retention of vitamin B1 depends on the amount of heat used during canning. Some vitamins and minerals may dissolve into the brine or syrup in a can during processing, but they retain their nutritive value if those liquids are consumed.

what is canning?

Canning is a preservation method that involves storing the food in airtight glass jars, then heating them to kill the microorganisms. During the heating process, the air is driven out of the container. Then, a vacuum seal is formed once the container cools down, preventing more air from getting in and contaminating the food inside. This process gives the food longer shelf life, typically one to five years (and sometimes even longer).Canning, by definition, is applying heat to food in a container with the purpose of removing air, thus creating a vacuum seal that inhibits natural spoilage that would otherwise occur. While our grandmothers may have had their own method for canning, today it is widely recognized that there are two safe and effective home canning methods: boiling water bath canning and pressure canning. Which method you use depends on the temperature needed to kill or deter the growth of harmful bacteria, yeast, or mold in an acidic or non-acidic environment.

Canning Methods

There are two major ways of preserving both low acid and high acid foods: water bath canning and pressure canning.Depending on the fruits, vegetables or meats you wish to can, choose the proper method and gain the ability to shop from your own pantry all year long.

Water Bath Canning

This method is ideal for high-acid foods like fruits, jams, jellies, tomatoes, salsas, pickles, chutneys, pie fillings, vinegar, and condiments. It involves immersing the food containers in a completely covered boiling water to cook for a specific amount of time.If you are just starting out with canning your crop, water bath canning is the perfect choice for making an assortment of pickles, chutneys, apple butters and cranberry sauces. A water bath canner is a large pot with a wood or wire rack on the bottom to prevent the jars from touching one another as the boiling water flows all around and underneath the jars. In the absence of a rack, clean cotton dish clothes can be packed around the jars. It is essential that the pot is deep enough so that 1 to 2 inches of boiling water can entirely cover the jars.

High acid foods for water bath canning

fruit jams and jellies

salsa

pickles

relishes

chutneys

Pressure Canning

For low-acid foods like vegetables, meats, seafood, and poultry, the pressure canning method is the only safe way to preserve them. The jars are immersed in water and cooked using a special pressure cooker. The above mentioned types of food can harbor a bacteria called Clostridium botulinum, and pressure cooking is the only way to kill it.Intimidation and fear is in the back of everyone's mind when they first encounter pressure canning. What if it explodes, what if someone gets sick?

And what if everything does work out according to plan?

If you want to preserve low acid foods, with a pH of more than 4.6, you'll want to invest in a pressure canner to ensure that you can heat the contents of a jar up to 240°F or more. The reason for doing so is to prevent the spores of botulism from growing.

A pressure canner is a cast-aluminum or stainless steel pot with a lid that locks, as well as having a pressure gauge.

Cooking under pressure allows the temperature of the boiling water to rise from 212°F (100°C) up to 240°F (116°C). Always follow the instructions that come with your pressure canner, and you will be off to a great start. Also, consult your recipe for processing times for each type of food. If you live 1,000 feet above sea level, you will have to adjust for your altitude.

Setting all inhibitions aside, pressure canning really is a

wonderful way to preserve food, but you may just need to try it to believe it.

Low acid foods for pressure canning

meats

poultry

seafood

potatoes

green beans

carrots

corn

beets

sweet peppers

pumpkins

Types of Pressure Canners

A dial gauge pressure

canner has a dial that indicates the pressure inside.

As heat and pressure increase inside the canner the dial rises.

Gauges may indicate each ½ or 1-pound increment; others mark only 5-pound increments leaving the user to determine the pounds in between.

A dial gauge allows the user to determine pressure increments for higher altitudes. At altitudes of 2,000 feet or below, pressure should be 11 pounds for meats and vegetables, and 6 pounds for fruits.

It is necessary to monitor the gauge and adjust heat when it is in use to maintain the correct pressure.

It is recommended that dial gauges be checked for accuracy each year. Contact your local Penn State

Extension Office for testing information

A weighted gauge pressure canner has a weight that controls the pressure.

One type of weight is a flat disk with 5, 10, and 15-pound markings.

Another type consists of three metal rings that sit on top of each other; for 5 pounds only one ring is used; an additional ring is added for each additional 5 pounds.

When the pressure inside a weighted gauge canner is reached, the weight will “jiggle" indicating the proper temperature inside.

Some weights jiggle 3 or 4 times a minute; others jiggle continuously. Consult the manufacturer's directions for the canner you are using.

Because you can hear the jiggles, you can monitor the pressure without being constantly beside the canner.

Weighted gauge pressure canners process meats and vegetables at 10 pounds pressure and fruits at 5 pounds pressure. At altitudes above 1,000 feet it is necessary to increase the pressure by 5 pounds.

Weighted gauge canners do not need tested for accuracy.

Boiling Water Canners

A water bath canner surrounds the jars of food with boiling water, transferring the heat into the jar of food. Fruits, acidified tomatoes, pickled products, and jams and jellies can be safely processed in a boiling water bath.

Jars need to be totally surrounded by the boiling water.

A rack is needed to allow water to circulate under the jars.

There needs to be space at the top of the canner so that jars can be covered with one to two inches of water.

The canner needs a lid.

A boiling water bath canner may be purchased, or you can create a water bath canner from equipment you already have. You need a pot that is deep enough so there is space for a rack, the jars, and at least one inch of water above the jars, and room for the water to boil rapidly without boiling over.

Atmospheric Steam Canners

Atmospheric steam canning is the latest method approved for home food preservation. Research conducted by the University of Wisconsin shows that steam in an atmospheric steam canner reaches the temperature of boiling water (212º F) and is safe for processing high acid foods the same as boiling water.

An atmospheric steam canner usually has a low base with a rack and a tall lid that fits over the jars.

The lid has one or two holes near the base that allows steam to escape.

The lid needs to be left in place and the canner heated to force air out of the canner until a column of steam forms that is 6 to 8 inches long. Steam is hotter than air.

Foods processed in boiling water can be safely processed in an atmospheric steam canner. Processing times are the same.

Canning Equipment

Canning jars, lids and rims

Canning jars, commonly known as mason jars, are created specifically for canning. They come in several standard sizes, including quart (4 cups), pint (2 cups), half pint (1 cup) and 4 oz (1/2c). The most common brands today are Ball and Kerr.

Standard sizes for canning jars: 4 oz, half pint, pint and quart

In case you're curious, from left to right: blueberry jam, sweet holiday cherries, salsa and spiced peaches.

The size you choose will depend on what you're canning and how much you'll need to use at one time. I use half pints and 4oz jars for canning jams and jellies; pint jars for things like salsa and pie filling; and a mixture of pints and quarts for things like canned fruit and tomatoes.

You'll also have a choice of two sizes of the opening at the top of the jar–regular or wide mouth.

Wide mouth vs regular mouth canning jar

You can use either type of opening for any canning recipe; the main difference is how easy it is to transfer food in and out of the jar. I like to use wide mouth jars when I'm canning large pieces of fruit, like peach halves, because they fit better through the opening. However, most of the time, the type I use depends on what I have on hand.

You can easily find canning jars at most grocery stores, hardware stores or big box stores. I prefer to look for canning jars at thrift shops, because they're pretty easy to come by, although you need to be a little more patient in building up your supply.

Canning lids are in two pieces, by the way. A lid and a rim. Did you know you're not supposed to keep rims on your jars after they're sealed? They can start to rust after a while. True story.

Two piece lid for canning

IMPORTANT NOTE: You can re-use jars and rims, but you should use a brand new lid every time you can something. Replacement lids can be purchased with or without extra rims.

Water bath canner

(or large pot with a lid, and a rack)

I use a large kettle that's made specifically for canning, known as a "water bath canner" which will can pint jars. I bought it at Menards for about $30, as I recall.

Water bath canner

It came with a rack that fits seven jars. I am able to can 4 oz, half pint and pint jars with this canner.

Jar rack for a water bath canner

If you aren't ready to buy a canner, you can simply use a large stock pot for small batch canning like I did when I started out. In most cases, you'll be limited to canning 4 oz jars and half pint quantities, but it's great for learning (and for small kitchens). In place of a rack, you can attach several jar rims together with paper clips and place it at the bottom of the pot, which will keep the jars from resting on the bottom of the pot. It's very important to have a rack in your canning pot; if your jars rest directly on the bottom of the pot, they can crack open.

I also have a larger canner that I bought at a killer garage sale for $5, which will accommodate quarts–these are more difficult to come by, so if you see one, snatch it up!

If you’re planning to can a food with low acidity, such as meat, corn and some vegetables, you will need a pressure canner. I’ve never done any pressure canning, so I can’t tell you if there are any extra tools needed. It’s on my list, though.

Jar lifter

While this isn’t technically “required equipment”, I’m putting the jar lifter in this section because it makes the process much easier, safer, and it generally costs less than three dollars. A jar lifter has a rounded end coated in rubber that will securely grab a mason jar when it's in the hot water so you can transfer it out of the canner without it slipping. You could get away with using tongs with rubber bands around the ends, but having used both, I'd highly recommend investing in a jar lifter. You won't be sorry.

Dutch oven or large stock pot

This is used for cooking the food that you will be canning. When it comes to this pot, bigger is better.

Mine is an enameled cast iron dutch oven, which is great because a) it's large, which means lots of surface area for recipes that require that the liquid evaporate, b) the cast iron heats more evenly than other types of metal and c) the enamel cleans up really easy.

A stir stick or chopstick

Have I stumped you on this one? What do you think it's for?

Before sealing your filled jars, you'll need to slide this little tool down the inside edges of the jar to get rid of little air bubbles. Chopsticks will do the job, I use one of these stir sticks–the one on the left is a glass swizzle stick (great name, huh?) and the one on the right is a naked lady drink stirrer that I brought back from a trip to Spain. As you can see, anything goes for this tool.

A kitchen timer

Everybody has one. The hardest part is remembering to set it when you are supposed to. (I adore mine; you can get it here.)

Kitchen tools used for canning

Wooden spoon

For mixing jam and jelly and stirring salsa...

Mixing bowls

Various sizes, used for mixing ingredients and holding fruit while you cut, peel and such. (Vintage Pyrex is my favorite.)

Sharp knives

I consistently use a paring knife (the smaller one) and a chef's knife when I'm preparing food for canning. The paring knife is for cutting off bad parts of fruit, peeling off skin and things like that. I use the chef's knife for quartering and chopping.

Tongs

When you're canning, tongs are like superman fingers for reaching into hot places without getting burned. I keep them handy for taking lids off pots and reaching into hot jars to readjust large pieces of fruit.

A slotted spoon

This is handy particularly for canning whole pieces of fruit or tomatoes where you need the liquid to drain off.

Lots of clean towels

Canning is messy! Wipe your hands, place hot jars on them so the jars don't ruin your countertop, clean up messes, and so on.

A strainer and/or cheesecloth

Useful particularly for making jelly when you need to strain seeds out of your mixture.

Ladle

For transferring food into your jars.

Oven mitts

Mine are connected in one long piece, which is more handy than you can imagine....I can't tell you how many times I think, “Now where is my potholder?” when I’m canning, because I drop it in random places in the kitchen. If the two mitts weren’t connected, I’d never find them. But that’s just me.

Benefits of Canning and Preserving Food

Canning and preserving protects food from spoilage so that it can be used at a later time. Some preserving methods, such as drying, date back to ancient times. Other methods, such as canning, are more recent. There's no doubt that being able to serve fresh tasting, home canned or preserved foods to family and friends throughout the year is definitely of labor of love.

Whatever food preservation is chosen -- canning, freezing or drying -- these efforts produce:

A pantry full of fresh, high-quality homegrown foods.

Having a pantry stocked with canned and preserved foods offer a cushion against the fluctuating cost of healthy foods. If you enjoy specialty foods from gourmet stores but dislike the high prices, home canning is a safe and economical way to preserve large or small quantities of high quality food.

Convenience.

Canning and preserving provides a pantry full of convenience foods that fit into busy lifestyles that your family love.

Confidence in the ingredients that go into food preparation.

If you like to control what ingredients go into your food preparation and want to know that they are fresh, canning and preserving your own food is the answer.

Protect your finances against inflation and rising food costs.

One of the main advantages of canning and preserving foods is taking advantage of fresh food when it's abundant. When food is abundant -- at harvest -- generally it means lower cost.

Creates a sense of accomplishment and relaxation.

Many people love working in the kitchen and handling food and get a sense of relaxation and love watching friends and family enjoy the products of their efforts which provides a great sense of accomplishment. Taking the time to select a recipe, choose and prepare the food, and package and preserve it for safety is fulfilling and a source of pride for the home canner. Nothing is more satisfying than looking at a pantry full of canning jars, or a freezer full of preserved food.

Having fun.

Producing canned and preserved foods in the kitchen is fun and easy -- and who doesn't love having fun.

Tips of the Art of Canning and Preservation

Pick Ripe Produce

Although you'll be adding sugar, salt, acid, and/or pickling spices to your fruits and veggies that will not only help prolong their life but complement or amplify their flavor, the star ingredient itself won't get any tastier than when you start out. This may seem obvious, but be sure to pick ripe, great-tasting berries, stone fruit, vegetables, and other raw ingredients or you'll likely be underwhelmed when you open your jars down the line. You can get away with using slightly overripe fruit for jams and jellies, but overripe produce won't make good pickles.

Know When to Get Creative

Normally, we're all for tweaking recipes and treating them more like templates than rigid rules, but when it comes to canning, it's important to follow the recipe exactly as written; even just adding fresh herbs can potentially throw off the delicate balance of acid, which can make your food spoil much more quickly. Luckily, you can find plenty of creative canning recipes online and in cookbooks dedicated to the subject. And if you just can't help yourself, see when and how you can safely tweak canning recipes, and what you must never alter.

Don't Use Your Instant Pot for Pressure Canning

Along the same lines, while we usually love finding new ways to use all our kitchen appliances—and while some Instant Pot models actually have a canning setting—the USDA advises against using it for pressure canning recipes. It may be safe to use for water bath canning recipes, but a pressure cooker is not the same as a pressure canner, and it's important you use the latter piece of equipment for pressure canning recipes.

You Don't Need to Buy a Water Bath Canner

That is, if you already own a large stockpot and a steamer rack, and as long as the pot is large enough to give you proper room; per the National Center for Home Food Preservation, it "must be deep enough so that at least one inch of briskly boiling water will be over the tops of jars during processing.

Always Use the Proper Canning Method

If a recipe calls for pressure canning, you must use that method; you can't decide to use the boiling water bath instead, because the temperature won't get hot enough to kill all the microorganisms and bacteria. The pressure canning method is used for low-acid food like vegetables (that have not been pickled first), beans, and meat. Water bath canning is appropriate for high-acid food like fruit and tomatoes, as well as veggies that have been pickled.

Be Sure to Sterilize Correctly

Sterilizing your jars is critical—the whole point of preserving food is to kill or inhibit the growth of harmful bacteria, after all. Many resources say you can use your dishwasher to sterilize jars, but that isn't actually considered adequate (at least not in all cases); to properly sterilize them, they need to be covered by boiling water for 10 minutes. That also means that if your recipe calls for processing the jarred food for at least 10 minutes or if you're pressure canning, you don't have to sterilize the jars first. It's still recommended that you warm the jars, but you never need to warm the lids.

Fresh Lemon Juice Isn't Best

This is another instance where we go against our usual ethos; fresh-squeezed citrus juice always tastes best, but the reason that bottled lemon juice is preferable in canning is that it's been pasteurized and the pH is consistent. There are some exceptions where you can use fresh lemon juice with no worries, but when in doubt, defer to your recipe instructions.

Pay Extra Attention to Pickles

When pickling produce before canning, there are a few extra things to be aware of: you should buy pickling salt (or know which brand of kosher salt and what amount can be substituted in its place); you need a vinegar that is at least 5 percent acid and should never alter the total amount (though you can add sugar to correct a brine that is too sharp). If you're using cucumbers, skip the waxy grocery store specimens, as the brine won't penetrate properly.

Practice Proper Mise en Place

Since canning usually happens in big batches and involves a significant amount of equipment and prep, it's even more beneficial than usual to get everything ready before you begin. Be sure to read your recipe all the way through, make sure you have the right amount of each ingredient on hand—but also check your supplies. Examine the canning jars for nicks, cracks, uneven rims, or sharp edges that may prevent sealing or cause breakage; check that the lids have no dents and that the sealing compound is even and complete; and check that the bands fit properly. Do this at least a few days ahead of time so if you do find issues, you can fix them before you have a mountain of fresh fruit in front of you.

slow cooker strawberry jam

Don't Overfill Your Jars

Overfilling jars can cause leaks and interfere with a proper seal, so be sure to leave enough headspace at the top—that is, some empty space at the top of the jar between the bottom of the lid and the contents. Each recipe will indicate the proper amount of headspace, so pay attention to that. If you underfill jars, that can sometimes cause sealing issues too, or may cause the top layer of the contents to discolor (which isn't dangerous, but isn't ideal). Read more about headspace here.

Don't Forget to Burst Your Bubbles

Similar to the above, when packing your jams and jellies into jars, you'll want to force out any air bubbles to help ensure the lids tightly seal. You can buy a special tool for this job, but a clean, sterilized chopstick is just as good for banishing bubbles, and a small, flexible spatula also works. Just don't use a metal knife.

Always Check Your Seals

After canning, whether you use the water bath or pressure canning method, check every single jar to make sure it sealed. Allow the jars to cool completely before removing the bands and pressing on each lid; if it has no give and you can't easily lift it off with your fingertips, it's good to go to the pantry or in the cupboard. Any jars that didn't seal properly aren't safe to store unrefrigerated. You'll need to empty the contents into a new, sterilized jar and repeat the canning process, or you can simply store the improperly sealed jars in the fridge (and eat the contents within a month or two).

Place a Barrier on Your Countertop for Cooling

Placing hot jars on a cool kitchen counter can cause breaks, so be sure to lay down kitchen towels or hot pads wherever you plan to cool your processed jars. (If you hear pinging sounds as they cool, don't be alarmed; that's probably just the seals forming and is a good sign.)

Don’t Store Jars with the Bands On

Those rings that screw the lid in place aren’t actually necessary once the canning process is complete and the jars have sealed. In fact, leaving them on can make them corrode, which will make them hard to remove later. Taking the rings off also lets you see that you have a proper seal, and that it’s not broken by any expansion of the contents during storage, which could be a sign of bacterial growth; if any lids do come off during storage, throw the contents of those jars away. (You will need the bands for holding the lids in place once you break the seal yourself, but in the meanwhile, you can also reuse the bands for other canning projects. Just toss them once they begin to show any signs of rust or other damage.)

If you're canning with Weck jars that use rubber sealing rings, glass lids, and metal clips, you can remove those clips once cooled too.

How and why canning works

We all use canned products in our daily lives, and manny of us enjoy making them our selves.

This instructable is intended as a basic introduction to canning methods, and to some of the science behind how it works.

The basic idea is of course to preserve food over time without having to refrigerate it. An added bonus is that you can prepare foods that are ready for eating, straight from the jar with no further preparation needed.

So how can we store food for years without going bad after only a few simple steps?

Why doesn't it rot?

Causes of Decay and How to Stop Them.

So what is it that causes food to degrade

in the first place?

The main culprits are bacteria, fungi, enzymes in the food itself, oxygen and loss of water.

Lets have a look at each of them.

Loss of water

is easily prevented by

canning. In an airtight container, there is simply nowhere for the water to go. Problem solved.

Oxygen

is a very reactive chemical, and it readily binds to many compounds in our food. This is called oxidation and is what makes oils and fat go rancid. By boiling foods before canning, we effectively remove free oxygen by replacing it with water vapor. By canning food in airtight containers, we keep oxygen from getting to it. There will always be some oxygen left, unless you chemically remove it with additives that bind oxygen. In most cases the amount of oxygen available in a jar of canned produce doesn't noticeably degrade it.

Enzymes

are active proteins that both build molecules and break molecules apart in all living tissue. Some of these enzymes remain active, even though the tissue is no longer alive. This will contribute to the degradation of some foods. There are several ways to stop enzymatic activity. All enzymes have a set of conditions required for them to function. This includes temperature, pH, salinity and other factors. Shift these conditions outside of the preferred range, and the enzyme will be slowed down or completely stop functioning. In canning we do this in several different ways. One is by boiling. The high temperatures during boiling causes the structure of many proteins to degrade, and kills the enzymatic activity. This change in protein structures is the main reason food changes texture after boiling. Another way to halt enzymatic activity is to lower the pH values in the food by adding vinegar, citric acid or lemon juice.

Microbes

are the main problem when it comes to preserving food. Bacteria and fungi thrive in basically anything organic. They produce enzymes that degrade the food, and in some cases they produce compounds that are foul tasting or toxic in the process. In the canning process we aim to kill or deactivate all the microbes in our food, and prevent new ones from entering by making airtight seals.

So how do you kill microorganisms?

Boiling takes care of most of them, but many bacteria and fungi produce spores that are highly resistant to heat. To make sure these spores don't just start growing again when the food cools down, we can take additional measures. If living conditions are not ideal, the spores simply won't germinate, and the food stays fine, even though it contains viable spores. There are two main groups of bacteria producing spores. One is the Bacillus. All species in this group need oxygen to grow, so by removing oxygen in the canning process, we effectively halt their growth. The other group is the Clostridia. They thrive without oxygen, and removing it actually enhances their growth. To keep them from growing, we need to do more.

The most well known destroyer of canned goods is Clostridium botulinum. It produces an extremely potent neurotoxin that can kill you. This is the very same BoTox used in very low doses in medical treatment and cosmetics. One way to halt the growth of C. botulinum is to keep the pH low. A pH below 4.5 is generally considered safe. Most fruits are acidic enough to achieve this without adding more acid, but to be sure, you can measure pH with a pH-meter or pH strips. For foods with higher pH you need to actively lower it with something like vinegar, citric acid or lemon juice. If you don't want the food to be sour, you simply have to kill the spores as well as the bacteria. As mentioned earlier, normal boiling does not kill the spores. You need higher temperatures. Boiling at 121°C kills most known bacteria and spores. Keeping this temperature for 3 minutes is usually enough to kill the spores of C. botulinum, but remember that it takes a while for the entire contents of a jar to reach this temperature. Water temperatures this high can only be achieved in a pressure cooker, and pressure cookers usually come with a table to determine how long boiling times you need for different volumes. As most of us don't have pressure cookers available, acidifying or pickling is the most common way to preserve canned food.

Sugar and salt preserve food by lowering the water activity. What essentially happens is that the sugar or salt creates osmotic pressure that draws water out of the cells of microbes and renders them unable to grow.

Containers

You can reuse jars

from food you purchase, but there are a few things to be aware of. First of all, these jars might not be tempered to tolerate the pressure and temperature differences in canning. This could make the jars crack. To minimize the risk of this happening, you should not use jars with visible chips, cracks or scratches in them. Jars like these often have a relatively small sealing surface compared to purpose made canning jars, so the seal may more easily be corrupted. The seal on the lids could also be damaged, so you might have to buy new lids. Reused jars like these are most suitable for canning jams and jellies, where an airtight seal is not of vital importance. Reused jars lack one of the features of canning jars. Canning jar lids are designed to lift when the internal pressure gets to high, and release air. This reduces the risk of jar breakage.

Purpose made

canning jars are naturally the best option, as they are tempered to take the normal heat differences in canning.

When cooling down warm jars, make sure to not place them on a cold surface like a stone or metal counter top. Also make sure they are not placed in a drafty location, as the air movement could cool down the outside of the glass to fast. One tip is to cover cooling jars with a towel. Do not attempt to cool down warm jars in the fridge.

Metal cans.

This is where the term canning comes from in the first place, and we have all bought food in metal cans. Closing the cans however, requires equipment that the ordinary home canner is not going to invest in, so cans are primarily used in industrial production.

Heat sealable plastic bags

is a different option. These bags are food safe, tolerate heat, and can be sealed airtight. They can be used for both water bath and pressure canning. For water bath canning, you can use bags intended for sous vide cooking. These bags are usually not made to withstand temperatures much higher than boiling, so for pressure canning, look for purpose made retort bags.

Heating Methods

Now, lets look at different methods of heating the food. This is where we actually kill the microbes present in our food, so it is the most important step.

There are different ways to go about this, depending on what you are canning. The methods will be explained in detail in the following steps.

Open pot canning: Can be used on food with a pH value below 4.5. This includes a wide range of fruits. This method is usually used on jams and jellies which contain relatively high amounts of sugar in addition to the acid.

Water bath canning: Can be used for the same food as mentioned above, and it has the added benefit that the food is sterilized after the jar is closed.

Pressure canning: Is the only way to go for food with higher pH values than 4.5. This includes meat, fish, fruits like peppers, pees and zucchinis, and root vegetables like potatoes and carrots. Tomatoes are fruits with variable pH, and might need pressure canning.

Open Pot Canning

Open pot canning is what was mostly done in previous times. It doesn't really refer to the pot where you prepare the food, but to the fact that the container is open after you have finished heat-treating your food. The principle is that you sterilize jars and lids by boiling them or leaving them in the oven. The food is boiled to kill microorganisms and poured directly into the hot jars. The jars have to be capped immediately to prevent microbes from entering. The residual heat from the food and the jar will in most cases kill any microbes that might enter before capping. This is not considered true canning, as the food is exposed to the environment after it is heat treated. This method should only be used on acidic foods where there is no danger of C. botulinum growth. The only advantages of this method are that it is quick, and reduces the chance of jars cracking if you are reusing old ones. The disadvantages are that there is a chance microbes will enter the container after heat treatment, and that these microbes are not killed by the residual heat of the food. You also have to handle very hot jars and food, and at the same time make sure everything remains sterile.

Water Bath Canning

Water bath canning can be done in two different ways. One is that you prepare the food by boiling, put it in cans, and then sterilize the cans in a water bath. The other is that the food is put into the jars raw, and the entire cooking process is done in the water bath. The jars should be closed, and put into a water bath that covers them completely with about 5 cm of water above the lids. The boiling times for different food is something you need to check, but for pre boiled, acidic food, 10 minutes of boiling usually does the trick. Use a canning rack or towel in the bottom of the pot to make sure the jars are not in direct contact with the bottom of the pot. Direct contact can make the jar crack and the contents can get burned. To avoid jars cracking, you can let them cool down in the water bath. Remove the pan from the heat, and let it sit until the water cools down. This only works for food where there is no danger of overcooking, like jams and jellies. Jars should otherwise be cooled down in room temperature. Keep them away from draft by covering them with a blanket or similar. Make sure to not put hot jars down on heat conducting surfaces like stone and metal counters. The main reason jars crack is differences in temperature between outside and inside that creates tension in the glass.

Pressure Canning

When dealing with non acidic food, pressure canning is the only way to go. High pressure is the only way to achieve the temperatures needed to kill the spores of C. botulinum in food.

There are different types of pressure canners. Some have valves that can be set to open at a certain temperature or pressure. Others have valves that are controlled by adding weights to them to determine release pressure. These pressure canners are calibrated to work at sea level, so if you are using them at higher altitudes, you have to adjust for this by tuning or adding more weight to release valves. All of this is stated in the instruction manuals for the canners.

The magic happens at 121°C. No bacteria or spore harmfull to humans can survive temperatures above this for any length of time. At 1atmosphere pressure, water boils at 100 °C. To keep it in a liquid state at higher temperatures require higher pressure.

Pressure canners usually come with instructions regarding cooking times for different types and volumes of food.

Ordinary pressure cookers can not be used for canning. They are normally not equipped with adjustable pressure valves or any way of monitoring the internal temperature.

Common Mistakes

There are some common mistakes in canning that are easy to prevent.

Improper seals.

- Check your jars before use. If the edges have scratches or chips, they most probably will not seal well. The same goes for the lids if they are reused.

- Make sure that the rims of the jars are clean before closing them. Wipe of any food that was spilled on the rim.

Improper heating.

- If your boiling times are to short, you are not going to kill all the microbes present.

- Make sure to remove all air bubbles when you fill the jars. This is easily done by carefully stirring with a glass or metal rod, or just a knife. Air is a poor heat conductor, and air bubbles can insulate parts of the contents of your jar from being properly heated.

Cracking jars.

- Check your jars for cracks and scratches before use.

- Don't expose them to sharp temperature gradients.

- Don't overfill jars. Some foods expand more than others when heated, and if the jar is to full, it may crack.

- Canning jar lids are designed to lift slightly when the air pressure inside gets to high, and release it. When the jars cool, the lids are sucked down and create an under-pressure seal. Not using propper canning jars increases the risk of jar breakage.

- Don't let the jars touch the bottom of your pot or canner. Use a canning rack or a towel underneath the jars.

Exploding canners.

-Yes, pressure canners can and do explode. The reason is usually a failing safety valve. Inspect your canner before and after use. Valves should be cleaned and on some canners lubricated. Working with high temperatures and high pressure is potentially dangerous, so don't be sloppy with the preparations.

Advantages and Disadvantages of canning and preservation

Advantages:

Helps saving money

Saves nutritional value

Can last for years

Do not require electricity or refrigeration to store

Preservative and pesticides free food

Off season availability

Can serve as a gift

Portable

You get control of what to can and what to add

Sense of satisfaction of having canned yourself

Disadvantages

Time consuming process

Initial start up cost of buying the equipments

Person should know which foods are high risk and which are low

Change in ingredient may require a change in processing

Canning machines are expensive

Growing your own vegetables or fruits to save extra for the purpose of canning may take time

conclusion

I can generalise my results to different situations. The implications of my findings were that canned foods contain preservatives and other additives that make them last longer. Different canned fruits and different brands put varying amounts of additives into their products. This makes different fruits and brands have varying shelf lives. Some fruits, whether natural or canned last longer than others. In conclusion, we can conclude that spoilage mayalso occur in canned foods. Spoilagein the cannedfood can be identify through physical state.Look closely at all cans before opening them. A bulginglid, or a dented or leaking can is a sign of spoilage. When you open it, look for other signs, such asspurting liquid, an 'off' odour or mould. Don't taste or use canned foods that show any sign ofspoilage. Throw them away immediately; they are not at all for consumption.Also, to ensure safety of food products, quality control/ assurance through routine microbiologicalexamination of food products for pathogens and spoilage organisms, confirmation of properpasteurization and checking of leakages in cans are required. such as sugar. However, generally speaking, canned fruits lasted longer than natural fruits. Overall, canned fruits lasted longer than natural fruits. This can be concluded as a result of preservatives contained in canned fruits.

www.ingramcontent.com/pod-product-compliance
Ingram Content Group UK Ltd.
Pitfield, Milton Keynes, MK11 3LW, UK
UKHW021921190726
13853UKWH00002B/775

9 798417 455568